THE
BATTLE OF TRENTON

Turning Points in American History

THE BATTLE OF TRENTON

Martin McPhillips

Silver Burdett Company, Morristown, New Jersey

Cincinnati; Glenview, Ill.; San Carlos, Calif.;
Dallas; Atlanta; Agincourt, Ontario

862116

Acknowledgements

We would like to thank the following people for reviewing the manuscript and for their guidance and helpful suggestions: David Williams, Professor of History, California State University; and Verna Mair, Library Consultant, Aldine Independent School District, Houston, Texas.

Cover: John Trumbull's painting "Capture of the Hessians at Trenton" ©Yale University Art Gallery

Title page: Currier & Ives print of Washington at the Delaware is from a private collection

Contents page: Photograph of cannon courtesy of the Smithsonian Institution

Page 37: Portrait of Thomas Paine courtesy of the National Portrait Gallery

Library of Congress Cataloging in Publication Data

McPhillips, Martin, 1950–
    The Battle of Trenton.

    (Turning points in American history)
    Bibliography: p.
    Includes index.
    Summary: Presents the events in the Revolutionary
War leading up to the Battle of Trenton and describes
that clash and its aftermath.
    1. Trenton, Battle of, 1776—Juvenile literature.
2. New Jersey—History—Revolution, 1775–1783—Juvenile
literature. 3. Washington, George, 1732–1799—Military
leadership—Juvenile literature. [1. Trenton, Battle of,
1776. 2. United States—History—Revolution, 1775–1783—
Campaigns] I. Title. II. Series.
E241.T7M36   1985   973.3'3   84-40382
ISBN 0-382-06823-8

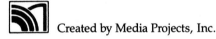 Created by Media Projects, Inc.

Series design by Bruce Glassman
Ellen Coffey, Project Manager
Frank L. Kurtz, Project Editor
Jeffrey Woldt, Photo Research Editor

CONTENTS

INTRODUCTION

THE CRISIS

On the riverbank, the tall Virginian sat down on a box that had once contained a beehive. Wrapped in his long cloak, he waited patiently, even though his plan was four hours behind schedule. The weather was growing worse. Heavy snow was falling, and the wind cut sharply across the Virginian's face. It was midnight.

From his seat on the box, the Virginian watched the long, black Durham boats arrive from the Pennsylvania side of the river. The Durhams had been specially built to carry iron ore. Tonight they carried scrawny, hollow-eyed men, eighteen artillery pieces, and several horses. The river was virtually uncrossable. The sailors manning the boats fought off large, sharp cakes of ice that raced toward them on the rapid current, ramming the sides of the Durhams.

George Washington

To the rebel soldiers who stepped out of the boats, the Virginian—their general and commander in chief—seemed determined, unemotional, and strong. He always seemed that way to the men. Though most of the men respected, even admired him, they had also heard rumors about the future of his command. There were whispers that he was not a great man after all, that he couldn't win a battle, let alone a war. It had been suggested that the Virginian should be replaced as commander, that a man with more military skill should get the job.

But there would be no job, no need for a commander in chief, if tonight's plan failed. The general had held these 2,400 men together for one final confrontation with the enemy. For four months he had been running from the British army. He could run no more. He had to win something. The future was on the line.

One of the most famous images from American history is this painting of Washington crossing the Delaware, by Emanuel Leutze.

Just a few days earlier the general confessed that the problems facing him might be more than he could handle. But at the same time, he drew up a daring plan. On Christmas night he would take his half-starved army across the Delaware River into New Jersey. While the troops the British had sent to occupy Trenton were recovering from their Christmas celebration, the general would strike them before dawn.

So now it was Christmas night. As the weather grew worse and freezing rain mixed with the snow, the general grew only more determined. The cold could not touch him, nor could the thought of turning back.

And on the ground could be seen the real evidence of the faith his men had in him. Bloody feet had left red trails in the snow. Several of the men were barefoot. The Continental Army had run out of shoes, but the shoeless were there, ready to march on to Trenton.

George Washington was a fine athlete and an excellent horseman. He owned a plantation in Virginia and was a modestly rich man. Twenty years earlier, while fighting in the French and Indian War, his horse had been shot out from under him in battle. Another bullet had torn through his coat. But he was never hurt. He had gained a reputation for being invulnerable.

George Washington had stepped off the Durham boats with one thought dominating his mind. That thought was the password given to the troops for this Christmas Night, 1776. The password was "Victory or Death."

SUPPLEMENT to the PENNSYLVANIA JOURNAL, EXTRAORDINARY.

PHILADELPHIA, *May* 19, 1766.

This Morning arrived Capt. WISE, in a Brig from POOL in 8 Weeks, by whom we have the GLORIOUS NEWS of the

REPEAL OF THE STAMP-ACT,

As paſſed by the *King, Lords* and *Commons.* It received the ROYAL ASSENT the 18th of March, on which we moſt ſincerely congratulate our Readers.

An Act to repeal an Act made in the laſt Seſſion of Parliament, entituled, *An Act for granting and applying certain Stamp Duties, and other Duties, in the* Britiſh *Colonies and Plantations in* America, *towards further defraying the Expences of defending, protecting and ſecuring the ſame ; and for amending ſuch Parts of the ſeveral Acts of Parliament, relating to the Trade and Revenues of the ſaid Colonies and Plantations, as direct the Manner of determining and recovering the Penalties and Forfeitures therein mentioned.*

 HEREAS an Act was paſſed in the laſt Seſſion of Parliament, intituled, *An Act for granting and applying certain Stamp Duties, in the* Britiſh *Colonies and Plantations in* America, *towards further defraying the expences of defending, protecting, and ſecuring the ſame; and for amending ſuch parts of the ſeveral Acts of Parliament relating to the Trade and Revenues of the ſaid Colonies and Plantations, as directed the Manner of determining and recovering the Penalties and Forfeitures therein mentioned:* And whereas the Continuance of the ſaid Act would be attended with many Inconveniencies, and may be productive of Conſequences greatly detrimental to the Commercial Intereſts of theſe Kingdoms; May it therefore pleaſe your moſt Excellent Majeſty, that it may be enacted; and be it enacted by the King's moſt Excellent Majeſty, by and with the Advice and Conſent of the Lords Spiritual and Temporal, and Commons, in this preſent Parliament aſſembled, and by the authority of the ſame, That from and after the Firſt Day of *May,* One thouſand ſeven hundred and ſixty ſix, the above-mentioned Act, and the ſeveral Matters and Things therein contained, ſhall be, and is and are hereby repealed and made void to all Intents and Purpoſes whatſoever.

1

THE ROAD TO WAR

On April 19, 1775, shortly after dawn, British troops fought with local militia composed mostly of farmers and shopkeepers in the village of Lexington, Massachusetts. The Royal governor of Massachusetts, Thomas Gage, had sent the troops to capture guns and ammunition that the Colonists were stockpiling near the village of Concord. The arms were intended for use in a rebellion against British authority. The direct cause of this seemingly minor skirmish can be traced back to events that took place a dozen years earlier.

In 1763, Great Britain found itself in serious debt. Its recent victory over France in the Seven Years' War (called the French and Indian War in North America) had drained the Royal treasury. The leaders of Britain decided that their American

Printed announcement of the British Parliament's repeal of the Stamp Act, May 19, 1766

colonies should help pay for the war. After all, one of the most important results of the victory had been that the French were now deprived of colonial rule in Canada and on the North American frontier. The colonists had benefited greatly from the war.

The first sign of trouble between Britain and the Colonies came with a series of new laws that fell under the single heading of the "Sugar Act." Passed by the Parliament in London, the Sugar Act caused the price of molasses in the Colonies to rise. This, in turn, badly affected the business of making rum, an important part of the Colonial economy. There was an outcry of opposition from Colonial merchants.

When news of the Colonial reaction reached London, it was greeted with surprise. Did not the Colonies exist for the benefit of the mother country? Determined to draw even more revenue from the Colonies, Parliament committed a serious blunder. In 1765 it passed the Stamp Act. This tax on legal documents, licenses, and publications took its name from the stamped papers that served as proof of payment.

The Colonies erupted in protest. The mother country had never taxed them before. For virtually one hundred and fifty years, since the founding of the first English settlement in North America in 1607, Britain had allowed her North American colonies an unusual amount of freedom. Each colony had its own legislative body to govern its internal affairs. But none of the colonies was allowed to send representatives to the British Parliament.

Patrick Henry, a powerful speaker, declared before Virginia's House of Burgesses that the Colonies must never accept "taxation without representation." The Colonists were British subjects, and as such they were entitled to the rights of British subjects. Without representatives in Parliament, Henry was saying, the Colonies could not be taxed legally. To the majority of the British Parliament, however, being a British subject meant that you obeyed British law and paid British taxes.

Patrick Henry delivering his address to the Virginia Assembly

The most serious argument between the mother country and her North American Colonies had begun. The Colonies wanted their traditional freedom from London's control. London seemed determined to curtail that freedom.

The Colonists won the first round in this dispute. They simply refused to pay the taxes due under the Stamp Act. When Parliament realized the taxes could not be collected, it repealed the Stamp Act in 1766. This was only a temporary victory for the Colonists. Britain sent word across the Atlantic that its right to tax the Colonies still existed.

In 1767, thinking that the Colonies objected only to interference in internal affairs, Parliament passed the Townshend Acts. The Townshend Acts put a tax on a variety of items—including paint, glass, paper, and tea—shipped to the Colonies from the mother country. The method of collecting these new duties on imports also transferred control away from local government and into the hands of Royal agents.

In 1768 the Massachusetts legislature denounced the Townshend Acts in a proclamation that was sent to the other twelve Colonies, along with a call for united action. This became known as the Massachusetts Circular Letter.

The response to this from the other side of the Atlantic was quick and harsh. The British prime minister dissolved the Massachusetts Assembly until such time as it chose to cease its opposition to the Townshend Acts. When other Colonial assemblies protested in support of Massachusetts, they too were dissolved.

Then an incident occurred that resulted in even harsher action by the British Crown. A ship belonging to John Hancock was seized by customs officials in Boston harbor. In response, groups of men from the port of Boston roughed up the officials and illegally unloaded the cargo from Hancock's ship. Then they pulled the customs collector's barge ashore, dragged it through the streets, and set it afire in front of Hancock's house.

The Crown knew that this open defiance of authority was extremely dangerous. The result was that in September 1768 Britain sent troops to occupy Boston. The result was an even more intense resentment by the people of Boston toward the British.

The incidents at Boston harbor and the dissolving of Colonial assemblies brought the first serious mention of armed resistance to British authority.

With Massachusetts under military occupation, the Colonial initiative switched to Virginia. In the House of Burgesses, a thirty-seven-year-old colonel of the Virginia militia stepped into the center of the controversy. George Washington restated the principle that the right to tax Virginians rested solely with Virginians. Then he denounced Britain for its

This engraving of the British landing at Boston harbor in 1768 was made by Paul Revere, the silversmith and engraver who became renowned for his "midnight ride" in 1775.

harsh measures in response to the Massachusetts Circular Letter. The delegates in the House of Burgesses backed Washington unanimously. An important Virginian, with a reputation throughout the Colonies as a military leader, had made his position clear. Washington stood with the cause of opposition to the Crown.

The next day the House of Burgesses was dissolved by the Royal governor.

In response, Virginia joined Massachusetts in agreeing not to purchase goods from Britain. These two in turn were joined by all but two of the remaining Colonies. This badly hurt British merchants, and in 1770 the Townshend Acts were repealed.

Britain again had backed off, as it had with the Stamp Act. The Colonies relaxed their position, allowing imports to flow in again from the mother country. But the issue of whether England could tax the Colonies was still alive. A small tax on tea remained to irritate the Colonists.

On March 7, 1770, another incident in Boston led to fresh opposition to the Crown's authority. An unruly crowd hurled sticks and snowballs at a British guard post. A squad of His Majesty's troops rushed to the scene. In the confusion, they fired on the crowd. Five men were killed. Although the crowd was probably just as much at fault as the troops, this tragedy again rallied public opinion against Great Britain. This was the famous Boston Massacre.

By 1773, three years later, the radicals in Boston were ready to use any issue that they could to stir up trouble. They didn't have long to wait. Tea, already a symbol of Britain's insistence that it could and would tax the Colonies, became the center of another controversy.

London had granted the East India

An engraving by Paul Revere of the Boston Massacre. One of the leaders of the rebel crowd was Crispus Attucks, who was part black and possibly part Indian. He is often said to be the first Colonist to die in the cause of independence.

Company the exclusive right to sell tea in America. Even though the price was kept low, the Americans disliked the principle behind this arrangement. When the Royal governor of Massachusetts, Thomas Hutchinson, showed bad judgment by appointing his brother-in-law and two of his sons managers of the tea, fresh protests erupted.

On December 16, 1773, a group of 180 radicals, dressed as Indians, boarded three ships in Boston Harbor and dumped 342 chests of tea overboard. This became known as the Boston Tea Party. Similar actions were taken in New York, Philadelphia, and Charleston, South Carolina.

The response to the Boston Tea Party arrived from London in May 1774, and it set off the final spiral toward war. Parliament closed the port of Boston to all ships. The British army and navy were directed to enforce the order. The port would be reopened only if the citizens of

Amos Doolittle's depiction of the battle at Lexington

"The Engagement at North Bridge, Concord," by Amos Doolittle

Boston paid for the tea that had been thrown into the harbor.

Other measures followed, including one that essentially took from Massachusetts the right to govern itself. These measures were known as the "Intolerable Acts." Other Colonies pledged support for Massachusetts. Again, Virginia took the lead, calling for a congress of representatives from all of the colonies.

In September 1774, delegates gathered in Philadelphia for the First Continental Congress. Beyond the expectations of even its most radical members, the Congress struck back hard at the

Crown. It banned all imports from Great Britain as of December 1, 1774. It also formed the Continental Association, which would oversee the ban. Every local government—city, town, and county— was to elect a committee to enforce the Association's policies.

In its efforts to exert control over the Colonies, Britain had brought together thirteen separate political units. Almost all of the representatives to that first Congress were strongly opposed to the idea of independence from the Crown, but the stage had been set for the great events to come.

Tensions grew more rapidly now. The gathering storm centered on Boston, where the port remained closed and thousands of men were left unemployed as a result. Many citizens of Boston and the surrounding countryside prepared to take up arms.

During the first months of 1775, guns and supplies were stockpiled in Concord. The British, commanded by General Thomas Gage, received reports of this growing cache of weapons. On the night of April 18, Gage ordered troops from Boston to march to Concord, find the arms, and seize them.

As the troops left Boston, Paul Revere made his famous ride through the night to warn citizens across the Massachusetts countryside. The British were on their way.

Shortly after dawn, the troops reached Lexington, where they encountered about one hundred militiamen. Here, amid confusion on both sides, the "shot heard round the world" was fired. It has never been clearly established which side the shot came from, but it was most likely fired by a Colonist. The British Redcoats quickly fired off several volleys. Eight Colonists were killed. One

Corinne Abbazia Hekker

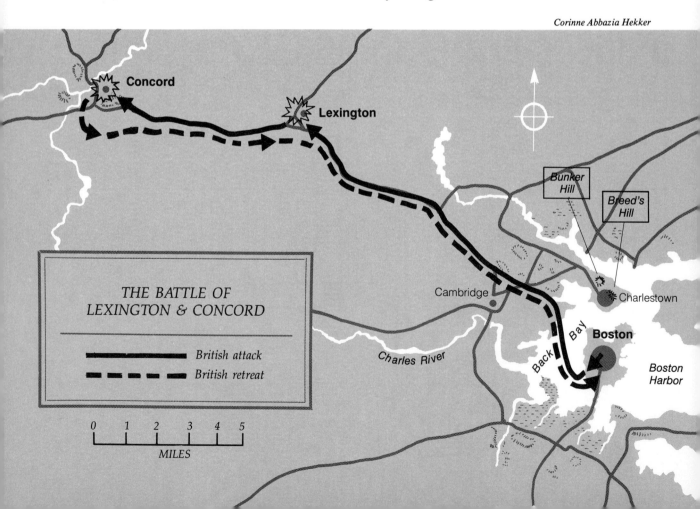

THE BATTLE OF
LEXINGTON & CONCORD

———— British attack
— — — — British retreat

0 1 2 3 4 5
MILES

Concord

Lexington

Bunker Hill

Breed's Hill

Cambridge

Charlestown

Charles River

Back Bay

Boston

Boston Harbor

British soldier was slightly wounded.

The Redcoats marched on toward Concord to search for the store of arms. There they encountered more Massachusetts militia, known as Minutemen, and the fighting grew heavier. The strong-willed Americans forced the British to retreat. Firing their muskets from behind trees and rocks, the militia tormented the Redcoats all the way back to Boston. The Americans proved to be poor marksmen, inflicting surprisingly light casualties for all the rounds they fired. Nevertheless, they had forced a sophisticated professional army to turn and run.

The Colonists' war for independence from Britain was begun.

2

THE WAR BEGINS

As the British retreated to Boston, hundreds of militiamen from across Massachusetts continued to answer the call to arms. Soon, Boston was surrounded by a wide arc of ordinary citizens loosely organized as an army. As night fell on the nineteenth of April, Boston was under siege.

In the days and weeks to come more men arrived from surrounding colonies. Old General Artemas Ward was placed in command of this amateur army. He faced the immediate problems of providing rations and pay, and settled disputes between contingents of men from different villages and towns.

As clumsy a situation as it was, this collection of men willing to fight for the cause of their own liberty inspired other men throughout the Colonies to prepare for rebellion. As early as May 10, 1775,

John Trumbull's painting shows the presentation of the Declaration of Independence to the Continental Congress.

rebels under the command of Ethan Allen and Benedict Arnold attacked and captured Fort Ticonderoga on Lake Champlain in New York. Arnold continued on and attacked two more British positions at Crown Point and St. Johns.

Back on the outskirts of Boston, General Ward was in the process of making a fateful move. On the night of June 16, he and his advisers sent a detail of men onto Charlestown peninsula above Boston to fortify Bunker Hill. So disorganized was the rebel chain of command that a mistake was made and the fortifications were dug on nearby Breed's Hill instead.

The next morning, the British general in charge of Boston, Thomas Gage, ordered an artillery bombardment of the rebels' new position. When this failed to drive them from the hill, Gage sent troops across the Charles River by barge to attack the fortification. In command of the landing force was Sir William Howe, who would soon succeed Gage as the senior British general in America.

More than two thousand Redcoats massed at the base of the hill. The forces were shuffled into position. Slowly, three deep, they climbed the hill in a full frontal attack on the rebel entrenchments. Showing cool courage and discipline, the Americans held their fire until the British line was only fifteen yards away. The result was deadly. The British turned and retreated back down the hill, leaving hundreds of bleeding dead and wounded sprawled on the hillside. A second assault produced equally bloody results,

with the Redcoats turned back again. When the third assault was mounted, the rebels were virtually out of ammunition. The British, their bayonets gleaming, took the hill. Most of the rebels, however, managed to retreat. American losses came to five hundred dead and wounded.

The British had captured the hill, which was militarily useless, and they had paid an extraordinary price. Nearly half of their attack force of some 2,200 were killed or wounded. It was one of the

"The Battle of Bunker's Hill," by John Trumbull

bloodiest moments of the war and a great psychological victory for the patriots. It has been suggested that the overly cautious manner in which Sir William Howe would later lead the British War effort resulted from his witnessing the slaughter of his men at Bunker Hill (actually Breed's Hill).

As important as the brave stand at Bunker Hill had been, something of even greater importance had taken place in Philadelphia the day before. The Second Continental Congress, having decided to declare the New England army around Boston a *Continental* Army, chose a commander in chief for that new American force. Washington was asked to take the reins of command.

In his acceptance speech, Washington told Congress he was uncertain that he was equal to the task. He was not just being modest. Though he had indeed gained valuable military experience twenty years earlier during the French and Indian War, Washington had never been formally trained in the art of European warfare. And now he was about to lead an army composed of farmers, merchants, and frontiersmen against the most powerful and professional war machine of the time. The master of Mount Vernon had good reason for his doubts.

It is hard to say exactly why Washington seemed so natural a choice for the job. He appears to have been a man blessed with qualities of character that earned the admiration of other men. He was not, for instance, a great speaker, but it was certain that he stood behind what he said. He was a man of privilege, a slaveholder, a prominent member of the Virginia elite. He could easily have withdrawn from the conflict to his beloved plantation at Mount Vernon. But the principle of self-determination and its long tradition in the Colonies was more important to him.

On July 2, two weeks after his appointment, Washington arrived in Cambridge, Massachusetts, to take charge of the Continental Army that surrounded Boston. He was forty-three years old and would remain in command for eight years, until he was fifty-one. No other general in American history has ever led an army at war for so long a time.

For the rest of the year 1775, Washington was mostly occupied in getting his ragtag troops into shape. The camps around Boston were a disgrace, and he ordered that they be cleaned up and properly maintained. There was very little discipline among the troops and even less respect for military authority. Such things went against the grain of their independent Yankee souls. Washington established an effective chain of command and brought order to the ranks. Through the force of direct honesty, dignity, and patience, he was able to get a body of officers and soldiers who were largely New Englanders to accept a Virginian as their leader. As a military commander he had much to learn, but as a leader he was already established.

This powerful aura of leadership was Washington's greatest natural gift. He was helped in this by his commanding physical presence. At six feet two inches he was much taller than the average eighteenth-century man. This physical stature was further enhanced by his superb horsemanship. No less important was his fairness in dealing with his men, and the great personal sacrifice he had made to become their leader. Officers and regular soldiers alike would come to respect him greatly and even to love him.

As the year 1776 began, Washington was eager to break the deadlock and take Boston from the British. But without enough artillery that action was not possible.

As would happen so many times throughout the Revolution, an inspired individual rose to the occasion. Henry Knox, a heavyset Boston bookseller who was self-educated in artillery warfare, completed a seemingly impossible task. He traveled to the captured Fort Ticonderoga and hauled back to Boston—across three hundred miles of ice- and snow-covered wilderness—fifty-nine artillery pieces. It was a thunderstruck British command that awakened on March 5, 1776. They looked up to the Dorchester Heights above Boston to find that during the night it had been fortified by men and heavy guns.

Henry Knox arriving at Boston with cannons removed from Fort Ticonderoga

Sir William Howe, the British general, ordered his troops to take the rebel position. Before the operation could get under way, however, a terrific storm hit. The sky blackened, rain poured down, and a gale of wind tore across the city.

After the storm passed, Howe thought better of his plan and canceled the attack. He then reached an informal agreement with Washington. If the American commander in chief would agree not to bombard the city, Howe would board his troops onto the British

Sir William Howe

fleet waiting in Boston harbor and set sail. Washington agreed and Boston was liberated.

Though he was no doubt pleased that the cause had advanced this far, Washington knew only too well that the British war machine was not yet even in gear.

The Hudson River in New York was the most vital waterway in the Colonies. Washington believed that the British soon would attempt to seize New York City to gain control of the mouth of the great river.

The commander in chief shifted the bulk of his army—now numbering close to twenty thousand men—to New York. On their arrival, the troops set about increasing the fortifications already begun under General Charles Lee and Lord Sterling.

For nearly three months the Americans waited anxiously for the British to make their appearance. Finally, on June 29, a massive British fleet sailed into the waters off New York Bay. The ships put troops ashore on Staten Island, where they set up camps. The waiting began anew.

A month passed. Near the end of July another fleet arrived with reinforcements from England. Then, early in August, another seaborne force arrived from the south. All told, a force of 32,000 was landed, consisting of British soldiers and Hessians, who were German mercenaries hired by the Crown to fight the Colonists. In addition, there were 10,000 seamen aboard the ships. This was the largest force Britain had ever sent out from its shores. There was no doubt that King George III, his ministers, and Parliament were deadly serious about putting down the rebellion in the Colonies.

While all this was happening, the rebellion took on a new, earth-shaking dimension. The Continental Congress had been hotly debating whether or not the Colonies should declare themselves free of British rule. A year earlier, such a suggestion would have met with stern disapproval from most delegates to the Congress. But now a thirty-three-year-old delegate from Virginia, Thomas Jefferson, had drafted a document that declared the Colonies free and independent. It was submitted to the Congress for consideration.

After much arguing and revising, the Congress approved Jefferson's document. On July 4, 1776, members of the Congress signed the Declaration of Independence. It dissolved the political bonds between the Colonies and Great Britain. It was the ultimate act of treason.

When the news reached New York, citizens there pulled down a lead statue of King George III. Later it was melted down and turned into ammunition for rebel muskets.

On Staten Island, as the hot days of August rolled by, British troops and Hessians prepared for action. During these long days and nights, the king's forces were tormented by mosquitoes.

A prophetic story emerged from those tormented camps. One night, several hundred British and Hessian soldiers crowded around a large bonfire. They were about to witness the burning of effigies—or dummies—of four rebel leaders, including one of George Washington. Just as the effigies were torched a thunderstorm erupted and sent the troops running for cover. After the storm passed, soldiers who returned to the site of the fire were shocked by what they saw. Three of the effigies had been consumed by the flames. But a fourth, the one of Washington, was untouched. To the Hessians this was a very bad omen.

It may well have been just that, for the British. Many times, the real George Washington would escape the flames of war. The commander in chief had a remarkable talent that few possess. Both he and his cause seemed able to survive against the worst of odds.

On August 22, the British launched their invasion. Fifteen thousand troops crossed by boat from Staten Island to Gravesend, on Long Island (today the southern shore of Brooklyn). A few days of bad weather intervened, and then more troops were sent across.

Alonzo Chappel's depiction of the Battle of Long Island

When the attack finally came, the rebel lines on Long Island were smashed. The British forced the Americans to retreat to Brooklyn Heights, behind the considerable earth fortifications that had been dug there.

General Howe, determined not to see a repeat of the horrors of Bunker Hill, ruled out a direct assault. Instead, he moved his men up gradually, having them dig trenches as they edged closer and closer to the rebel position.

Washington was with his troops in the fortifications. At first he was determined to make a stand, but he eventually became convinced that to do so would spell disaster. His only hope was to get his entire army out of Brooklyn, back across the East River, onto Manhattan Island.

But if Howe were to realize that this was Washington's plan, he could move quickly to cut off the escape route. He would be able either to destroy or to capture Washington's army. Washington, however, had learned something from having fought Indians in the French and Indian War: If men could move in darkness, they doubled their advantage by doing it quietly.

Without alerting the enemy, boats were gathered to the Brooklyn shore of the East River. Through the night of August 29 the rebels were ferried across the river to Manhattan. The boats, buffeted by rain, wind, and rough waters, dropped their passengers and returned for another load. Howe did not realize what the enemy was up to until after dawn on August 30. By then it was too late to do anything about it.

If this failed to help Washington's reputation as a fighter, it made his name as an escape artist. To this day, the night retreat from Brooklyn is recognized as a great military maneuver. The commander in chief had led his army out of a dangerous trap. In this case, sheer survival was a great achievement. Victory would have to wait for another day.

Nevertheless, the battle of Long Island had cost the Americans dearly. More than a thousand men had been captured, hundreds killed or wounded.

Back on Manhattan, an unruly rebel army now questioned the ability of its leaders. Overconfident before the fighting began, the troops had swung over to the other extreme, perhaps believing that they would never have a chance against the British war machine.

Now, while the rebel spirit was shattered, was the time for Howe to strike Manhattan. But again the British commander dragged his feet. He waited two weeks, until September 15, to land his force at Kips Bay, on the east side of the island. Meanwhile, Washington withdrew most of his army to encampments on Harlem Heights, in the northern part of Manhattan Island.

On the 16th, the Americans met the

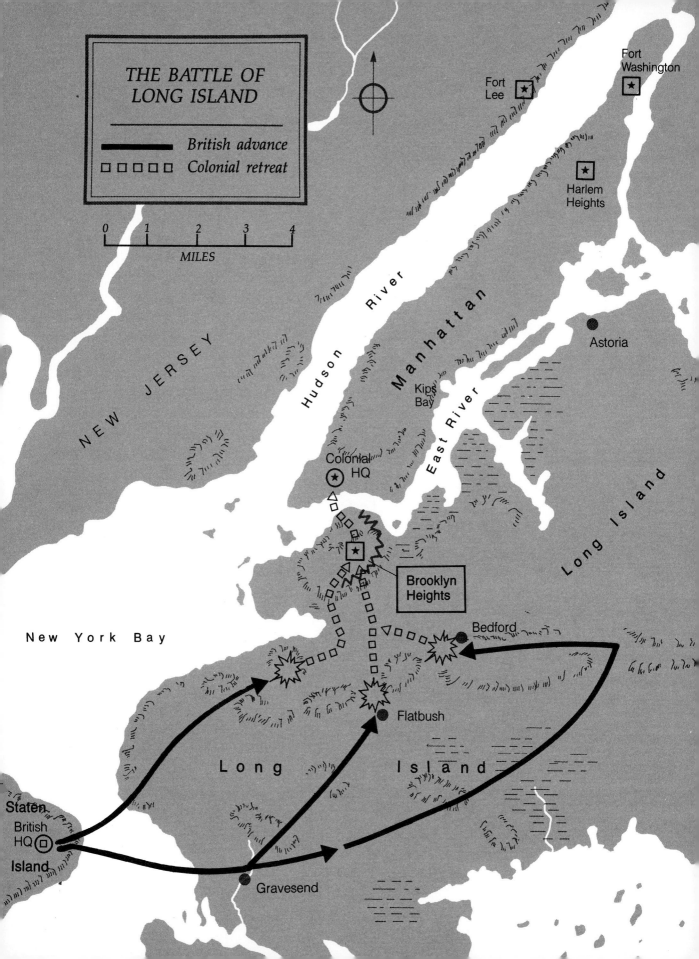

THE BATTLE OF LONG ISLAND

━━━━━ British advance

□ □ □ □ □ Colonial retreat

0   1   2   3   4
MILES

Fort Washington

Fort Lee

Harlem Heights

Hudson River

NEW JERSEY

Manhattan

Astoria

Kips Bay

East River

Colonial HQ

New York Bay

Brooklyn Heights

Bedford

Long Island

Flatbush

Long   Island

Staten
Island

British HQ

Gravesend

The skirmish at Harlem Heights as rendered by Alonzo Chappel

British advance guard in a brief engagement near the heights. Surprisingly, the rebels overwhelmed the enemy, forcing them to retreat. This minor victory raised rebel spirits and may have caused Howe to become even more indecisive.

Washington held on at Harlem Heights for a few weeks, but during the first half of October, on the advice of his officers, he left Manhattan. The army that marched north into Westchester was a crippled shadow of the eager force that had come down from Boston months earlier. Then they had had a fresh cause to drive them on. But where was their cause

now? Increasingly, it was Washington himself who embodied the meaning of the rebellion. The great man was still there, outwardly calm, determined.

The only position in Manhattan not abandoned was Fort Washington, located on the Hudson near the northern end of the island. A garrison of about three thousand troops was left behind to hold the fort. This turned out to be the worst mistake that Washington made during the war.

Slowly but ominously, Howe pursued the retreating rebel army. The British scored a minor victory in the village of

White Plains, in Westchester. But Howe again faltered. He failed to pursue the main American army as it retreated to nearby North Castle. The Americans were revived by fresh supplies and by their reasonably good efforts in Westchester.

In early November, the British marched back to Manhattan. The American command misread this as a plan to campaign into New Jersey. Instead, on November 16, Hessians stormed Fort Washington, capturing the troops, artillery, and supplies there. More than 2,500 men were taken prisoner. It was a terrible blow, and Howe followed it up by taking Fort Lee, on the New Jersey bank of the Hudson, across from Fort Washington. More men were captured, and, between the two forts, staggering amounts of arms, ammunition, and other supplies were lost.

The commander in chief, shaken by the twin defeats, took his main army and fell back through New Jersey. Howe sent the vigorous Lord Cornwallis after Washington with a large force. Cornwallis did not hesitate, as Howe so often did. But by now Washington was used to showing his back and running. He managed to stay a step ahead of the only British general who seemed determined to chase him. Just as Cornwallis sent his advance guard into Newark, for instance, Washington's rear guard was pulling out.

Finally, on December 7, Washington began moving his troops from Trenton across the Delaware to Pennsylvania. The last men were ferried over on the 8th, just as Cornwallis arrived in Trenton. Washington, worried that Cornwallis would come after him, ordered all the boats on the New Jersey side either burned or brought over with the army to Pennsylvania.

Two things happened that would lead to a change in fortunes. First, Washington feared that the Delaware would soon freeze and the British army could simply march across it and seize Philadelphia, the rebel capital. Second, Howe apparently decided that it was time to stop fighting for the winter. He ordered that a line of outposts throughout New Jersey be fortified with men, who would spend the winter holding these posts.

Washington felt his back against the wall. Howe was determined to sit pat with what he had. The Colonial commander was tired of running. The British commander was tired of chasing. Winter was closing in, and the rebel army—Howe hoped, Washington feared—was close to disintegration.

The stage was set for Washington's desperate attempt to survive. To him this meant he must regain the initiative. He drew up plans to attack Trenton.

3

VICTORY OR DEATH

Colonel Johann Rall, commander of the Hessian troops holding Trenton, had worried for days that the rebels were up to something. Small rebel parties had been crossing the Delaware and pestering his patrols, often killing one or two of his men at a time. Rall also had received information that Washington had called a war council on December 22. At that council, Rall knew, plans for an attack had been discussed.

At the same time, however, Rall also learned about the condition of Washington's troops. He knew that they were half starved and exhausted. That knowledge and the increasingly cold and harsh weather helped put Rall's mind at ease.

So, on Christmas night, Rall had relaxed enough to attend a party at the home of Abraham Hunt, a Trenton merchant. His troops also celebrated the holiday with food and drink in their quarters.

Portrait of Lord Cornwallis by the English painter Thomas Gainsborough

Rall was busy playing cards and drinking when one of Abraham Hunt's servants handed him a note. But Rall must have held a good hand. He paid no attention to the note and stuffed it unread into a vest pocket. The note was from a farmer loyal to the Crown. It was a warning that the rebel army was on the move.

Outside, the weather was growing more severe. Snow and freezing rain were falling harder, driven by a sharp wind. Over on the Pennsylvania side of the Delaware, at a crossing point called McConkey's Ferry, the deep, booming voice of fat Henry Knox cut through the storm.

Knox was in charge of loading men, artillery, and horses onto the forty-foot-long Durham boats. The boats were under the command of John Glover and his men, the Marbleheaders (from Marblehead, Massachusetts). It was Glover who had been in charge of the boats on that night in August when Washington

Opening page of the first of Thomas Paine's pamphlets in the series titled The Crisis, *with its famous opening line, "These are the times that try men's souls." There were sixteen pamphlets in the series, published between 1776 and 1783. The pamphlet pictured above was published in December 1776, less than a year after publication of Paine's most famous work,* Common Sense.

had slipped his army out of Brooklyn Heights.

Waiting patiently on the New Jersey shore for the crossing to be completed was the commander in chief. The operation was well behind schedule. It was to have been completed by midnight. But it would be 4 A.M. before Glover's men were finished. The plan called for the attack to take place just before dawn. But with the delay it would have to go forward in daylight. There was still a nine-mile march from the landing point into Trenton.

Far downstream, below Trenton, two other units were also attempting to cross the Delaware. Near Bristol, Colonel John Cadwalader had been able to get 1,800 men across the icy river. Then it became impossible to bring his two artillery pieces over, and the colonel recrossed the river, working under the assumption that Washington himself had no doubt turned back. The other contingent, under General James Ewing, was supposed to cross near Bordentown and close off the escape route from Trenton to the south. Ewing made an attempt, but as the weather and the condition of the river grew worse, he gave up.

In the face of the terrible weather and the long delay, Washington remained fiercely determined. His men, already stretched to their limit, now faced the burden of a night march over the icy roads and through the pounding storm.

As they trudged through the snow, Washington rode up and down along the column, urging his men onward. "Press on, press on, boys!" he called to them. To stop and rest would be a fatal mistake. A few soldiers who did lie down fell asleep and never awakened.

It took two hours to reach the small village of Birmingham, a trek of some four miles from the ferry. At Birmingham, the troops split up into two columns. Washington went with the column that took the Scotch Road. Nathanael Greene would lead these men into the streets of Trenton. Greene was eventually to be recognized as Washington's most capable general. It was no coincidence that the commander in chief wanted him nearby at this important moment. The other column was led along the River Road by General John Sullivan.

The plan called for the two columns to converge on Trenton at the same time. Around the time they separated, Sullivan sent word to Washington that many of the men with him had discovered that their gunpowder was wet. Sullivan feared their weapons would be useless. Washington's reply was short and firm: "Use the bayonet. I am resolved to take Trenton."

At about 8 A.M., the column led by Washington and Greene approached the Hessian advance post. This was located about half a mile outside Trenton. As the storm continued to rage, the two sides fired on each other. The small contingent of about two dozen Hessians realized they were outnumbered, and they ran. Three minutes after the first shots were fired, Washington heard gunfire from the direction of the River Road. Sullivan's column had arrived on time.

The Hessians were now alerted, but there was much confusion in their ranks. Rall was awakened, and he made an attempt to assemble his men on King Street. But the rebels had moved quickly on the town. Henry Knox rolled his artillery into position at the north end of the street. As Rall shouted orders to his men, Knox raked the street with grapeshot.

General Nathanael Greene

The Hessians were carefully trained professional soldiers. They fought as a unit, and moved and fired and charged under the precise commands of their officers.

The Colonists, on the other hand, were undertrained amateurs. What fighting skills they had had come from battling Indians, tree to tree and rock to rock. From the beginning of the war they had trouble with the disciplined tactics of professional warfare. But now, as they rushed the streets of Trenton, it was their style of fighting that prevailed.

After taking a beating in the streets, the Hessians under Rall retreated to an apple orchard just outside town. They attempted to form lines for a bayonet charge back into Trenton's streets. But the rebels continued to press them hard, and the Hessian lines again fell apart. Colonel Rall was seriously wounded and soon fell from his horse. Some of his men helped him away from the battlefield to a Methodist church on Queen Street.

Another regiment of Hessians had retreated to the Assunpink Creek. The rebels were holding the bridge across the creek, which was the Hessians' only safe route of escape. The only other route was through the water, which was neck deep and dangerous. Some Hessians tried the creek and made it; some tried but didn't make it.

Their commander fallen, their escape routes cut off by rebel contingents, the

General John Sullivan

Hessians in the apple orchard surrendered. The Hessians trapped at the Assunpink held out a little longer. A Colonial officer sent word to their commanding officer that he would blow them to pieces if they didn't surrender. That was a convincing argument, and this group of Hessians laid down their arms.

Washington, who had watched the battle from high ground above the town, now rode down King Street. On the way he was met by Major James Wilkinson, who reported the Hessian surrender to the commander in chief.

The effect of Common Sense

Even at the outbreak of the Revolution, the notion of independence from Great Britain was not taken seriously by many in the Colonies. Most Colonists considered themselves British subjects and were proud of it. The rebellion against British authority was principally a protest against what the Colonists considered violations of their rights as Englishmen.

Thomas Paine

What changed the minds of many Colonists about loyalty to Britain was a political pamphlet titled *Common Sense*, published in January 1776. Thomas Paine, the author, attacked the belief that the American Colonists either needed or benefited from attachment to the mother country. He argued that the Colonies would be subjected to continuous involvement in European wars, of which there had been and would be many. Paine insisted that America would be far better off if it were independent of British rule. It would owe loyalty only to its own internal political system, yet it could have all the benefits of trade with European countries.

Common Sense made its case well enough to convince important Colonial leaders that independence was not a farfetched notion.

"Small islands not capable of protecting themselves are the proper objects for kingdoms to take under their care; but there is something absurd in supposing a continent to be perpetually governed by an island. In no instance has nature made the satellite larger than its primary planet; and as England and America, with respect to each other, reverses the common order of nature, it is evident that they belong to different systems: England to Europe, America to itself."

"America is only a secondary object in the system of British politics; England consults the good of *this* country no further than it answers her *own* purpose."

"O! ye that love mankind! Ye that dare oppose, not only the tyranny but the tyrant, stand forth! Every spot of the Old World is overrun with oppression. Freedom has been haunted round the globe. Asia and Africa have long expelled her. Europe regards her like a stranger, and England has given her warning to depart. O! receive the fugitive [freedom], and prepare in time an asylum for mankind."

Not wanting to jeopardize their first real triumph, Washington and his officers decided to withdraw to their camps on the other side of the Delaware. As they prepared for the return trip, the results of the battle were tallied.

Some forty Hessians had been killed, and about as many wounded, and nine hundred were taken prisoner. The Colonists, by most accounts, lost not a man, with only four wounded, although at least three men froze to death on the road to Trenton and on the return trip across the Delaware. Among the few Colonists wounded was an eighteen-year-old lieutenant named James Monroe, who forty years later would become the fifth president of the United States.

Before leaving Trenton, Washington observed a gentlemanly custom of war and visited Colonel Rall on his deathbed. The Hessian commander asked that his men be treated kindly. Washington promised that they would be.

It is interesting that when Rall's men removed the dying colonel's uniform, one of them discovered the note that Rall had stuffed, unread, into his pocket on Christmas night. The soldier showed the note to Rall, who commented that had he read it when it was delivered, he would not be where he was now.

Trenton was the first victory for Washington's army, coming after a long period of humiliation. Word of the success spread quickly through the Colonies. Hopes that only a few days earlier had been so dim were suddenly reignited. The cause seemed not to be fading after all.

Washington, although fully aware of the symbolic importance of the Trenton victory, had no illusions about its military impact. His back was still against the wall. His troops were still in horrible condition, without enough sleep, food, and clothing. But, even so, he was eager to strike the British again, and soon.

Meanwhile, the British command was furious. Lord Cornwallis canceled his trip to England, and Howe quickly sent him into New Jersey with orders to "bag the fox." (The British generals had begun to refer to Washington thus.)

On the morning of December 30, Washington led his bedraggled army across the Delaware again. Even though this crossing was made during daylight, it was even more difficult than the first trip. Ice conditions on the river had worsened, and the day was brutally cold.

The army that went with Washington on the second crossing was about half the size of the army of the first crossing. The fighting force had been reduced by exhaustion, sickness, and desertion. They marched back to Trenton, where they took up position below the town on the south bank of the Assunpink.

Washington himself was not sure what his next military objective would be. He had another problem to deal with

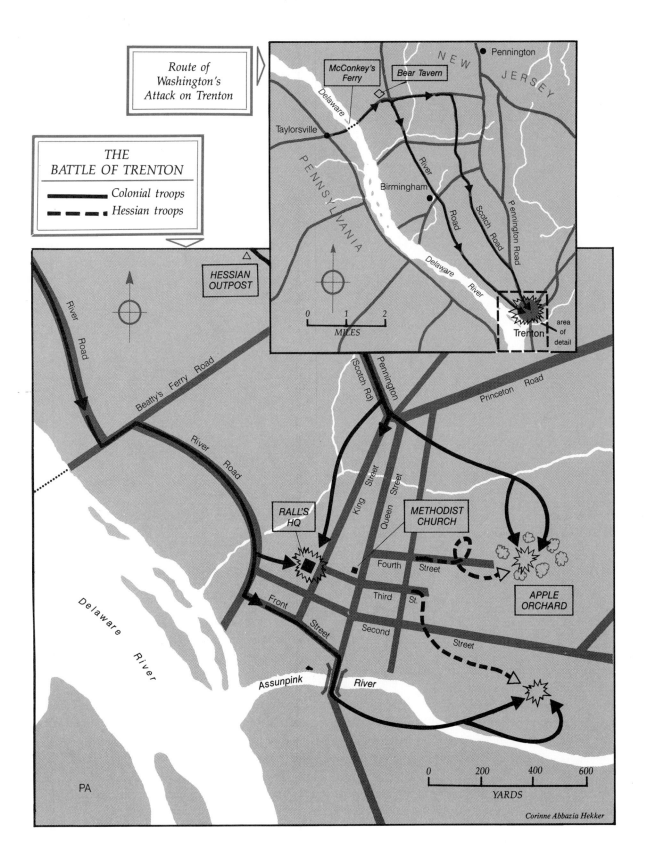

Route of
Washington's
Attack on Trenton

THE
BATTLE OF TRENTON
——— Colonial troops
– – – Hessian troops

Pennington

NEW
JERSEY

McConkey's
Ferry

Bear Tavern

Delaware

Taylorsville

PENNSYLVANIA

Birmingham

River

Scotch Road

Pennington Road

Delaware River

Road

area
of
detail

Trenton

0   1   2
MILES

HESSIAN
OUTPOST

River
Road

Beatty's Ferry Road

River

Road

(Scotch Rd)

Pennington

Princeton   Road

King   Street

Queen   Street

RALL'S
HQ

METHODIST
CHURCH

Fourth   Street

APPLE
ORCHARD

Third   St.

Front

Second   Street

Street

Delaware   River

Assunpink   River

PA

0   200   400   600
YARDS

Corinne Abbazia Hekker

39

first. In twenty-four hours most of his men could go home, their enlistments having expired. He had to do something to keep his army together.

The commander in chief called for one of the New England regiments to assemble. He rode on horseback before the men and asked them to stay six weeks longer. He spoke in a manner described as "most affectionate" by a soldier who was present. Washington rode to the side as drums beat for volunteers. Not one man stepped forward.

Washington was stunned. Suddenly he jerked his mount back to the front of the ranks and spoke to his men.

"My brave fellows," he said, "you have done all I asked you to do and more than could be reasonably expected. But your country is at stake, your wives, your houses, and all that you hold dear.

"You have worn yourselves out with fatigues and hardships, but we know not how to spare you. If you will consent to stay only one month longer, you will render that service to the cause of liberty and to your country which you probably never can do under any other circumstances. The present is emphatically the crisis which is to decide our destiny."

Washington was not a great speaker, but by his manner he had a way of moving men beyond personal concerns. Gradually, most of the men who were well enough to continue stepped forward. At other locations, officers called upon their regiments to stay. All told, most of the army agreed to remain for six weeks more. In return, Washington promised to pay each man a special bounty for staying. He did so without the permission of the Continental Congress, which might decide not to pay the bounty. But Washington was prepared to back up his pledge with his own resources.

On the final day of 1776, Washington received important news from the Congress. It had voted on December 27 to grant him new powers that essentially made him a military dictator. He could now raise more troops on his own and take whatever supplies he needed wherever he might be. He could arrest those who would not sell him provisions. The Congress had untied the commander's hands, knowing full well that the prudent Virginian would not abuse his expanded powers.

The new powers, however, would be of little help in the immediate dilemma. Cornwallis was on his way. By New Year's Day he was in Princeton, eleven miles above Trenton, with a force of eight thousand men. His objective was to end the war by destroying Washington's army once and for all.

On January 2 Cornwallis left Princeton before dawn, headed directly toward Trenton. Because the weather had suddenly turned warm on New Year's Day, with continuous rain, the road from

French musket used during the American Revolution. Although France did not formally ally itself with the Colonies till early 1778, the French supplied the Colonists with arms and other matériel as early as 1775.

Princeton to Trenton was a mess. The British were forced to march through knee-high mud. And as difficult as it was to march, moving the artillery was even more difficult.

In addition to the condition of the road, Cornwallis was slowed by continuous harassment from Colonel Edward Hand and his men. Firing from behind trees and rocks, Hand's men several times forced the British to form battle lines and bring up their big guns. But each time the British were ready to fight, Hand's troops would fall back. British artillery would rake the woods, but the rebels were already out of range. Hand kept up these tactics all the way into Trenton.

Hand's delaying action was extremely important. Washington, who was still not sure what he was going to do, wanted to make sure that night fell before Cornwallis could attack the Colonial position. The rebels were dug in on the south bank of the Assunpink and were flanked on their left by the Delaware. If the British were to overrun their lines, the Americans could find themselves trapped, with their backs to the great river. Washington and his officers were also concerned that Cornwallis might attack their vulnerable right flank.

Washington got the delay he wanted, in any case, as Cornwallis set up camp for the night at the north end of Trenton. While Henry Knox kept the British occupied with artillery bombardment, Washington held a war council. At the council, Washington once again decided to use his most polished talent—the disappearing act. If he had been able to get his army out of Brooklyn Heights, then he could certainly get out of harm's way from the south bank of the Assunpink.

This time, however, he was not planning a retreat. Throughout the night, the British kept close watch on the rebel encampment. They could hear the rebels digging and see their bonfires, and they had to take cover from the occasional artillery round. Cornwallis planned to assault the American lines at dawn and destroy what was left of Washington's army.

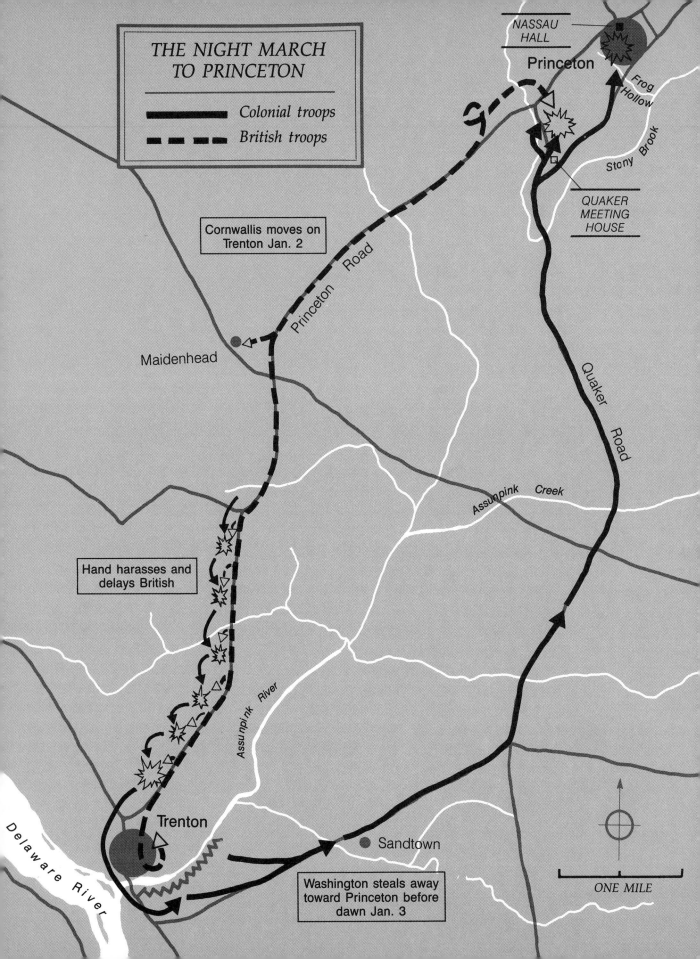

THE NIGHT MARCH
TO PRINCETON

——— Colonial troops
- - - British troops

NASSAU HALL

Princeton

Frog Hollow

Stony Brook

QUAKER MEETING HOUSE

Cornwallis moves on Trenton Jan. 2

Princeton Road

Maidenhead

Quaker Road

Assunpink Creek

Hand harasses and delays British

Assunpink River

Delaware River

Trenton

Sandtown

Washington steals away toward Princeton before dawn Jan. 3

ONE MILE

But when morning came, an amazed Cornwallis discovered that there was no fox to bag. Washington was nowhere to be found. Smoldering bonfires and well-dug earthworks were all that remained. The rebels had slipped away quietly under cover of darkness.

Through the night, the rebel troops struggled along a difficult back road. Washington was driving to strike the British garrison at Princeton before dawn. Like the Christmas-night march on Trenton, however, the plan was behind schedule. When day broke, the rebels were still two miles outside Princeton.

As Washington pressed on toward the town with his main army, he sent Hugh Mercer with about 350 men to destroy a bridge. The bridge was on the main road from Trenton, and destroying it would slow down the return of Cornwallis from Trenton.

When Mercer neared his objective, he was seen by the enemy. By coincidence, a sizable contingent of British were already on the road to Trenton. Cornwallis had left them behind the day before with orders to join him at Trenton the next morning. They were doing exactly as ordered when they were alerted to the

"The Death of General Mercer at the Battle of Princeton," by John Trumbull

presence of Mercer's force.

Soon enough, the battle was in progress. The British regulars formed ranks and, without much trouble, overran the rebels with a brutal and bloody bayonet charge. Mercer himself was trapped, beaten, and run through with a British bayonet.

Mercer's men fled in terror, but their retreat was halted by the appearance of Washington and the main rebel army. Washington took quick control. "Parade with us!" he urged the disorganized troops. "There is but a handful of the enemy, and we will have them directly!"

The rebels formed a long battle line, and Washington rode up to the front of the formation. He was going to lead this battle himself.

Leading his line forward toward the British, Washington ordered the men not to fire until he gave the command. Within thirty yards of the enemy, Washington ordered them to halt and then to fire.

Instantly, the British returned fire. Several seconds passed before the clouds of smoke cleared. No one knew whether Washington, who was in the direct line of fire, was still alive. But when the smoke cleared, the commander was still in his saddle, calm and unhurt. One of Washington's aides, John Fitzgerald, had even covered his eyes so that he would not see the general die.

Immediately, Washington waved the rebel line forward. The British broke ranks and ran. The rout was on. Washington could not resist the opportunity. He rode off after the enemy, waving his sword and shouting to his men, "It's a fine fox chase, boys!" The old soldier had never so inspired his troops as he did now.

One young officer who was there described the scene to his wife in a letter, writing, "I shall never forget what I felt at Princeton on his account, when I saw him brave all the dangers of the field and his important life hanging as it were by a single hair with a thousand deaths flying around him. Believe me, I thought not of myself."

Washington, who quite properly had always stayed behind the lines, had now demonstrated as much heroism in battle as any man had in the war.

Meanwhile, as Washington and his men disappeared in pursuit of the enemy, his generals turned their attention to capturing the British garrison in the village of Princeton. Many British troops fled the town, but those who couldn't get out took refuge in Princeton College's Nassau Hall. A very young lieutenant, Alexander Hamilton, helped bring up artillery to blast this final Redcoat stronghold. Amusingly, a cannonball decapitated a portrait of King George II that hung inside the hall.

The remaining British soldiers soon surrendered, and the victory at Princeton was complete. Two to three hundred Brit-

"The Battle of Princeton," by William Mercer

ish had been killed and another three hundred were taken prisoner. Only about forty rebels had been killed, but that unfortunately included some of Washington's best officers. It had been a short but bloody battle.

About two hours later, Cornwallis and his army were seen on the main road, returning from Trenton. There was no chance that Washington's own weary army—which had been on the go for forty-eight hours—could defend Princeton against the British advance. Also, Cornwallis was as angry as a hornet.

Washington's vanishing act at Trenton had left him hungry for revenge. The British were in a fitful state, "running, puffing, and blowing, and swearing at being so outwitted."

True to form, just as the British advance guard entered one end of Princeton, the last of the Americans were departing at the other end. Cornwallis sent some troops after the rebel army. For a while these units engaged the rebel rear guard, but the Americans fought off the attack and continued on.

4

VICTORY

After riding out of Princeton, Washington and his officers paused at a fork in the road. They considered yet another strike, this time at New Brunswick, a British supply base.

Washington knew that there was a war chest in New Brunswick containing some seventy thousand British pounds. The commander very much wanted to capture that chest, but one careful look at his troops convinced him that they hadn't enough strength for another battle. His officers agreed. The men could hardly walk, let alone fight.

It was decided to retire to the heights at Morristown, New Jersey. There the army could establish a winter base reasonably secure from attack. The Morris-

Charles Wilson Peale's painting of Washington, Lafayette, and aide-de-camp Tench Tilghman at Yorktown, 1781. In his left hand Colonel Tilghman holds the dispatch announcing victory to the Continental Congress.

town heights was actually a plateau that could be reached only by steep, rocky roads.

As news of the victory spread, the hopes of the people who supported independence were raised. Even though reports of Princeton and Trenton were greatly exaggerated, the positive effect of the triumphs was undeniable. Within days an increasing number of new recruits joined New Jersey's militia. This reversed a trend that had brought that colony dangerously close to a passive acceptance of British occupation and rule.

On the other side, the British were embarrassed and worried. The Crown's expectations of swift and sure victory in this war had been frustrated. The civilian populations of the Colonies had not rushed to support the King's army, as British leaders had thought they would. And now, after Trenton and Princeton, Howe lost confidence in his ability to hold New Jersey. He withdrew his troops from all but the two central New

Jersey towns of Perth Amboy and New Brunswick.

Of greater importance, Washington had shown that a hit-and-run strategy could work against a polished professional army. It was slowly dawning on both sides that fighting on the undeveloped North American continent, composed largely of farmlands and wilderness, was not the same as fighting on the more developed and more densely populated European continent. And it was now clear that the Continental Army knew how to attack as well as retreat. Neither Washington nor his men lacked the will to fight. The cunning night march out of Trenton and around Cornwallis's lines was hailed in Europe as a brilliant military stroke. For the first time, the notion occurred to military minds in Europe that the rebels could win. Such an idea had been considered laughable just a few months earlier.

But it was Washington, secure now in his Morristown stronghold, who underwent the greatest change. He knew now that he must avoid meeting his powerful enemy on its own terms. He could not yet win their kind of battle. He must use his mobile army and his hit-and-run tactics to dictate the terms of battle. He must stay out of fights that he could not win, such as the near disaster on Long Island.

For the future, the commander in chief would rely on surprise attack, patient waiting, defensive tactics, and con-

General Washington's camp chest

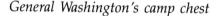

tinual harassment of the enemy's rear guard.

As the spring of 1777 came on, Howe tempted Washington to bring his army down into the New Jersey flatlands for battle. Washington didn't oblige. Howe marched his troops back and forth in New Jersey, hoping for a confrontation that would not come. The British, however, were plagued by the ever-increasing numbers of local militia.

Frustrated by all this, Howe finally decided to pull out of New Jersey entirely. He moved the troops back to the original base on Staten Island. This had only the most positive effect on the rebel cause. The king's army had given up territory it had spent great time and effort to take.

Success on this level, however, did not relieve the basic problems that plagued Washington. He would still complain to the Continental Congress—often to the point that its members became seriously annoyed with him—that he was short of men, weapons, rations, medical supplies, uniforms, and, always, money.

The war would not be decided for five more brutal years. King George III and the British Parliament could not tolerate the thought of losing their North American Colonies. But now the Continental Army knew how to bounce back from defeat and how, finally, to win.

Throughout the summer of 1777, Washington waited for a sign as to where the British would strike next. Howe had put his troops aboard the British fleet and sailed from New York. The fleet's destination was not clear.

By late August the mystery was over. The fleet sailed into Chesapeake Bay. Howe planned to land his troops there and then march them overland to Philadelphia. The British commander would then take the rebels' capital city. This move did not surprise anyone.

General Howe followed his victory at Brandywine with a successful surprise raid on Continental troops at Paoli, Pennsylvania, near Yorktown, in September 1777. The painting is by Xavier Della Gatta.

On September 11, Washington and Howe sent their armies against each other at the Battle of Brandywine Creek, west of Philadelphia. It was a decisive victory for the British. The Americans were overrun and forced to retreat.

After much maneuvering and some minor fighting, Howe sent Cornwallis into Philadelphia on September 25 to seize the rebel capital. The Americans offered no resistance. On paper, the British could claim a great victory. But in reality they had gained a city inhabited largely by women and children. Washington's

army was intact and recovering well from the Brandywine mishap. The Continental Congress had relocated at York, Pennsylvania.

Washington, meanwhile, prepared plans for a major offensive. Placing field command in the hands of the two generals who had led the rebels against Trenton, Sullivan and Greene, the commander in chief unleashed another surprise attack. This time the target was the British army garrisoned at Germantown, outside Philadelphia.

After marching all night, the rebel

"The Battle of Germantown," by Xavier Della Gatta

"The Surrender of General Burgoyne at Saratoga," by John Trumbull

army began its assault at dawn on October 4. At first it appeared that the rebels would win a smashing victory as they forced the Redcoats back, inflicting losses. But poor timing—brought on by a misunderstanding of the local geography—and heavy fog prevented victory. The rebels wound up firing on one another through the obscuring mists. The British rallied and counterattacked. The Americans retreated.

Although Washington's reputation at home suffered from this defeat, the at-

tack was hailed in Europe as a great achievement. European leaders were amazed at the quickness with which the Colonists had pulled themselves together after Brandywine, at the boldness shown in attacking the main British army, and at the new levels of organization achieved by the rebel army.

The most decisive rebel victory of the war so far was to occur far away from Washington and his main army, however. On October 17, Major General John Burgoyne, the leader of Britain's northern

"The March to Valley Forge, December 19, 1777," by William T. Trego

campaign, surrendered to General Horatio Gates at Saratoga, New York. Five thousand British and Hessian troops laid down their arms.

The cause of independence had turned the corner. The once laughable notion that farmers and shop owners could defeat the British professionals was now an established fact.

The great gains made by the Continental Army, capped by victory at Saratoga, helped promote a crucial change in world politics. As Washington and his men settled into winter quarters at Valley Forge, in Pennsylvania, France allied itself with the Colonies. On February 6, 1778, Louis XVI, king of France, signed a treaty pledging military support.

Meanwhile, the initial misery of Valley Forge gave way to a modest upturn in comfort and provisions. And something of great significance occurred at that snow-covered encampment. Baron von Steuben, a Prussian officer sent to America by Benjamin Franklin, began to drill the rebel troops in basic military disciplines. His well-meaning outbursts of temper and humorous insults charmed the tough rebels, and they took eagerly to his teachings. Von Steuben succeeded in molding the men into a far more efficient and professional army than Washington could have hoped for in 1776. Another step had been taken toward mastery of the British.

The spring of 1778 brought two important developments. First, Sir Henry Clinton took over command of the British forces from William Howe. Second, because France had allied itself with the rebels, the British decided to attack the French territory in the Caribbean. The war in North America was temporarily put on hold. Clinton was ordered to evacuate Philadelphia, demonstrating how little importance the occupation of the rebel capital actually had.

In mid-June, Clinton moved his long column of troops across the Delaware into New Jersey. Their destination was New York. After much disagreement among Washington's officers at councils of war, it was decided to attack Clinton's army. Unfortunately, Washington was compelled by military etiquette to give field command to his senior general, Charles Lee, who had recently been released by the British after more than a

The Marquis de Lafayette and General Washington at Valley Forge

Painting by Edward Abbey of Baron von Steuben drilling Washington's army at Valley Forge

year as a prisoner of war. Lee was an energetic defeatist who refused to believe that the rebel troops had any hope for success against the great British army.

Consequently, in the sweltering heat of June 28, Lee botched the entire action. He failed to support troops that had already engaged the enemy. His armies marched and countermarched without direction or leadership.

The Battle of Monmouth, in New Jersey, was developing into a disaster for the Americans. The troops, essentially without leadership, began a retreat. Onto this scene, however, charged the real leader.

Just as he had done at Princeton, Washington took over the field command.

Washington angrily dismissed Lee from command and then halted the retreat. The Marquis de Lafayette described the way Washington rode along the lines and reversed the tide of the battle: "Cheering [the soldiers] by his voice and example [he restored] to our standard the fortunes of the fight. I thought . . . that never had I beheld so superb a man."

As Washington reorganized the lines for battle, the troops demonstrated what von Steuben's training had accomplished. Now it was the rebel army that moved with smooth precision and discipline. All through the afternoon the two armies met in brutal conflict. Men from both sides collapsed in the near-one-hundred-degree heat.

Finally, Clinton withdrew, and the battle slowed to a conclusion. Charles Lee's incompetence had nearly cost the Colonists a defeat. As it was, Washington's action salvaged a standoff.

Lee's refusal to follow direct orders from Washington, based on his lack of confidence in his own troops, led to a court-martial and his dismissal. From the beginning of the war he had been one of the commander in chief's most unbending critics. He had told, and often convinced, many officers and influential people that he was Washington's better in military matters. But now, after Monmouth, his career was ended.

Monmouth was the last major en-

Emanuel Leutze's painting of Washington at Monmouth, relieving General Charles Lee of his command

gagement in the north. Hoping for a change in their luck, the British moved their main army to the south. Under Clinton, they captured Savannah, Georgia, in December 1778. Then, in May 1780, Charleston fell, and 5,500 rebel troops were forced to surrender.

Lord Cornwallis was given command of the British army in the south. During the spring of 1780, he established a chain of outposts in South Carolina. But, one by one, these posts were retaken by rebel raiders, led by men like the famous "Swamp Fox," Francis Marion.

In December 1780 General Greene took command of the southern army. Greene was extremely aggressive and made good use of the hit-and-run tactics that had succeeded so well in the north. Though technically he lost most of the battles, Greene's efforts eventually crippled Cornwallis's army.

Finally, in October 1781, Cornwallis was trapped at Yorktown, Virginia, by a combined force of Colonists and their French allies. After enduring a withering artillery bombardment, Cornwallis sent a letter to Washington asking for terms of surrender. Agreement was reached, and the formal surrender took place on October 19, 1781.

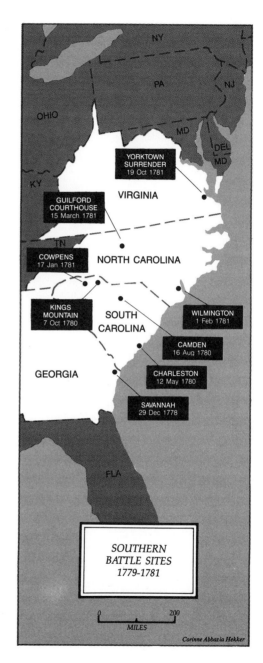

SOUTHERN
BATTLE SITES
1779-1781

Corinne Abbazia Hekker

York, Virginia 17th Octr. 1781

Sir

I propose a Cessation of Hostilities for Twenty four hours, and that two Officers may be appointed by each side to meet at Mr. Moore's house to settle terms for the surrender of the posts of York & Gloucester. I have the honour to be

Sir

Your most obedient & most humble Servant

Cornwallis

His Excellency
General Washington
&c. &c. &c.

AFTERWORD

THE LONG ROAD HOME

Although Yorktown was the final show-down, the war did not end formally until April 19, 1783, when the Continental Congress ratified a treaty of peace with Great Britain. This came precisely eight years after the first shots had been fired at Lexington and Concord.

Washington continued in command of the army until the last British troops left New York. Then, on December 4, 1783, Washington said farewell to his officers at Fraunces Tavern, on Pearl Street in New York City.

It was an emotion-charged occasion. Barely able to speak and unable to hold back tears, Washington told the officers, "With a heart full of love and gratitude, I now take leave of you. I most devoutly wish that your later days be as prosperous and happy as your former ones have been glorious and honorable."

Cornwallis's letter to General Washington, dated October 17, 1781, asking for a cease-fire and for a meeting to discuss terms of a British surrender

Each man came forward and embraced his commander. "Such a scene of sorrow and weeping I had never before witnessed, and hope I may never be called upon to witness again," wrote one of the officers present.

Washington crossed by barge to New Jersey. On his way to Philadelphia, where he would surrender his command to the Congress, he followed a path similar to that of his painful retreat from New York in 1776. Along the way he passed again through Trenton, where he had led a band of "half-starved scarecrows" to a victory that saved the cause of independence.

The time from the end of the Revolution in 1783 to the inauguration of Washington in 1789 is known in American history as the "Critical Period." It was during this time that the former colonies had to begin the task of forming a wholly new, independent government. Basically, the governments of the individual colonies that existed before the Revolution—the Colonial legislatures, courts, and governorships—served as the model for the newly independent states. In addition, the states together agreed to unite in a "firm league of friendship" under the Articles of Confederation, which were ratified in 1781. The Articles provided for a national government, but one without much authority.

Washington and others—notably Alexander Hamilton—were worried by the years of weak union under the Articles. They feared the states would become divided over their interests, resulting in turmoil within and aggression from Europe. Washington lent his considerable influence to the holding of a Federal Convention—later known as the Constitutional Convention—and served as its president during the summer of 1787 in Philadelphia.

A new charter of government, the Constitution, was ratified by the states in 1788, and Washington was elected the first president of the United States. He served two four-year terms before retiring in 1797. His eight years as president were often as turbulent as his years as commander of the Continental Army had been. But under his leadership, a new government had made the transition from idea to reality. That reality, pursued with iron will on that frozen Christmas Night of 1776, is today our heritage.

INDEX

Page numbers in *italics* indicate illustrations

SUGGESTED READING

FLEXNER, JAMES THOMAS. *George Washington in the American Revolution*. Boston: Little, Brown, 1968.

_____. *Washington: The Indispensable Man*. Boston: Little, Brown, 1974.

HOFSTADTER, RICHARD, ed. *Great Issues in American History: From the Revolution to the Civil War, 1765–1865*. Part I: Revolution and Independence. New York: Vintage Books, 1953.

KETCHUM, RICHARD M., ed. *The American Heritage Book of the Revolution*. New York: American Heritage Publishing Co., 1958.

_____. *The Winter Soldiers*. Garden City, N.Y.: Anchor Books, 1975.

2 3 4 5 6 7 8 9 10—JDL—93 92 91 90 89 88 87 86